COMMUNITY · CONNECTIONS

HOW DO THEY HELP?
OXFAM INTERNATIONAL

BY KATIE MARSICO

Published in the United States of America by Cherry Lake Publishing
Ann Arbor, Michigan
www.cherrylakepublishing.com

Content Adviser: Rob Fischer, Ph.D., Professor and Director, Master of
Nonprofit Organizations, Jack, Joseph, and Morton Mandel School of Applied Social
Sciences, Case Western Reserve University
Reading Adviser: Marla Conn MS, Ed., Literacy specialist, Read-Ability, Inc.

Photo Credits: © Sjors737 | Dreamstime.com - Health Care For Kenyan Babies, Nairobi Photo,
cover, 1, 19; © think4photopop/Shutterstock, 5; © John Wollwerth/Shutterstock, 7;
© Evans/Thinkstock, 9; © Hulton-Deutsch Collection/CORBIS, 11;
© Chung Sung-Jun/Thinkstock, 13; © Asianet-Pakistan/Shutterstock, 15;
© Joseph Sohm/Shutterstock, 17; © Christopher Furlong/Thinkstock, 21

LIBRARY OF CONGRESS CATALOGING-IN-PUBLICATION DATA
Names: Marsico, Katie, 1980- author.
Title: Oxfam international / by Katie Marsico.
Description: Ann Arbor, Mich. : Cherry Lake Pub., 2016. |
Series: Community connections: how do they help? | Audience: K to Grade 3. |
   Includes bibliographical references and index.
Identifiers: LCCN 2015048733| ISBN 9781634710527 (hardcover) |
   ISBN 9781634711517 (pdf) | ISBN 9781634712507 (pbk.) |
   ISBN 9781634713498 (ebook)
Subjects: LCSH: Oxfam—History. | International relief—Juvenile literature.
Classification: LCC HV553 .M277 2016 | DDC 362.5/577—dc23
LC record available at http://lccn.loc.gov/2015048733

Cherry Lake Publishing would like to acknowledge the
work of The Partnership for 21st Century Learning.
Please visit www.p21.org for more information.

Printed in the United States of America
Corporate Graphics
CLFA11

OXFAM INTERNATIONAL

CONTENTS

HOW DO THEY HELP?

WORKING TO END WORLD POVERTY

In 2015, two devastating earthquakes struck Nepal, a country in South Asia. More than 9,000 residents died, and hundreds of thousands lost their homes. Survivors faced starvation, disease, and homelessness.

Oxfam International was committed to aiding the Nepalese people. This organization delivered

Oxfam International helps communities recover from disasters like this one.

Think about the many problems people face following a natural disaster. For example, how do they practice good **hygiene** without fresh water? How do you think they care for crops and farm animals? How do they stop illness from spreading?

5

food and fresh water to victims. It helped them rebuild and plan a future not overshadowed by **poverty**.

Oxfam International is made up of 17 separate **humanitarian** groups. Together, they work to end poverty and social injustices in more than 90 nations.

Oxfam International helps communities set and achieve long-term goals to end poverty. They think that no one should live without food, basic services, or opportunities to succeed.

Access to clean water is essential to a healthy community.

LOOK!

Go online and look for a list of all of the organizations within Oxfam International. Next, search for a map that shows where Oxfam International is active. Finally, try to look for information about programs that your community helps support.

THE ORIGINS OF OXFAM

The roots of Oxfam International stretch back to World War II (1939–1945). During that conflict, Great Britain's naval forces stopped food and other supplies from reaching enemy troops in Greece. This military action led to **famine**. Residents of Oxford, England, decided they had to do something to end the suffering of innocent people.

Poor farming conditions can cause famine, as well.

ASK QUESTIONS!

Want to know more about World War II? Which nations were involved in this conflict? How did World War II draw attention to international human rights? Visit the library, go online, or talk to your teacher to learn the answers!

9

In 1942, British citizens formed the Oxford Committee for Famine Relief, or Oxfam. Members of Oxfam **lobbied** the British government to ease its naval restrictions. They succeeded in delivering food aid to women and children in Greece.

In the decades that followed, people set up branches of Oxfam outside of England. These **nonprofit** groups assisted communities around the world that were being challenged by hunger and poverty.

Helping to feed people who are hungry is just one way to help those affected by poverty.

Are you able to guess how Oxfam International pays for its programming? You're correct if you said that some funding comes from governments and separate humanitarian groups. Private donations and money earned through fund-raising are additional sources.

In 1995, various Oxfam groups united to form Oxfam International. By joining forces, they hoped to have a more powerful impact on poverty. Today, Oxfam International continues to provide emergency supplies and services to communities in crisis. It also campaigns against social injustices such as unfair trade agreements and unequal opportunities for women and girls. Oxfam International recognizes that these problems often go hand in hand with poverty.

Oxfam International strives to effect social change on a global scale.

G20
leaders
must
fight
poverty

☺ Oxfam ⊕ OBOS
One-Body One-Spirit Movement

G2

정상
빈곤
싸우
합니

☺ Oxfam

THINK!

The different groups within Oxfam International are all nonprofit organizations. They sometimes work with government leaders and other public officials. Yet they themselves are not part of one specific government. Do you think this is important? Why or why not?

13

To successfully aid people in more than 90 countries, Oxfam International depends on both volunteers and paid staff. Some work as lobbyists. They push for laws that are designed to protect the poor and end **discrimination**.

Oxfam International also relies on nurses, doctors, translators, and educators. **Economists**, scientists, engineers, and experts on farming and land usage are other examples of Oxfam workers.

Children in communities that struggle with poverty often need medical attention.

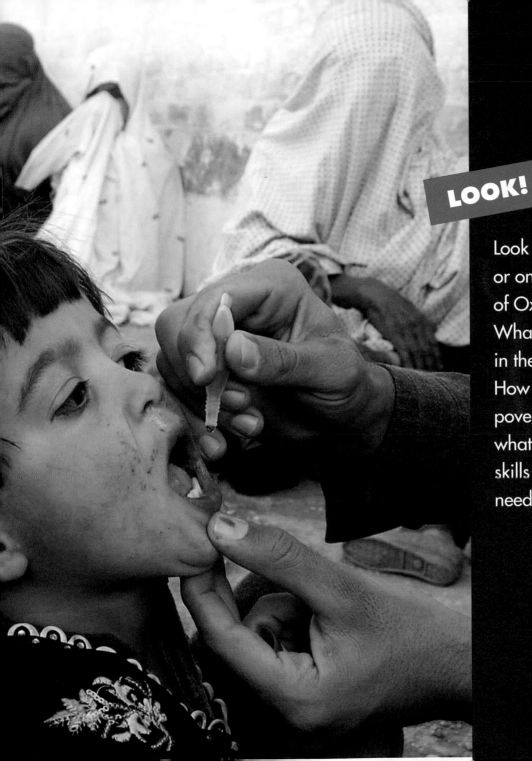

LOOK!

Look at the library or online for photos of Oxfam workers. What are the people in the pictures doing? How are they fighting poverty? Based on what you see, what skills do you think they need to possess?

15

BUILDING BRIGHTER FUTURES

There are several ways that Oxfam International helps people overcome poverty. In some cases, it offers immediate assistance to communities that have been devastated by violence or a natural disaster. Oxfam International supplies residents with food, clean water, medicine, hygiene kits, and donations of money. Workers also construct shelters and try to

When homes are destroyed by natural disasters families need help with more than just building supplies.

Are you able to guess how many people Oxfam International helps each year? (Hint: Recent studies suggest that it's a big number.) If you guessed between 20 million and 21 million, you're right!

17

keep local farms and businesses running as smoothly as possible.

Oxfam International also gives people the means to permanently avoid poverty. For instance, it ensures that farmers in developing communities are paid a fair market price. Oxfam International supports the creation of schools and health care programs, too. It also raises awareness about how issues such as climate change affect the world's food supply.

Communities with established health care systems can thrive.

How do climate changes caused by pollution affect farming and food production? What else impacts Earth's food supply and how it is distributed? Search online or contact Oxfam International for answers to these and other questions.

19

Finally, Oxfam International educates the public about social injustices. It campaigns against laws and business practices that fail to provide people with equal opportunities. Thanks to its efforts, individuals and groups facing discrimination have a stronger voice and a chance to succeed.

Oxfam International offers hope to communities struggling to escape poverty. It empowers men, women, and children across the globe to improve their lives.

20

Children all over the world, from America to Africa, benefit from Oxfam International programs.

CREATE!

Create a magazine about Oxfam International! Research ten of its programs and write fast facts about each one on a separate sheet of construction paper. Draw pictures, too. Finally, staple the pages together and share with your friends.

GLOSSARY

discrimination (dis-krim-ih-NAY-shuhn) the practice of unfairly treating a person or group of people

economists (ee-KAH-nuh-mists) people who study how goods and services are produced, bought, and sold in a particular area

famine (FAM-in) a situation in which large numbers of people don't have enough to eat

humanitarian (hyoo-man-ih-TER-ee-uhn) relating to people who work to improve the lives and living conditions of others

hygiene (HYE-jeen) the things people do to keep themselves and their surroundings clean in an effort to stay healthy

lobbied (LAH-beed) sought to influence lawmakers or public officials on a particular issue

nonprofit (nahn-PRAH-fit) not existing for the main purpose of earning more money than is spent

poverty (PAH-vur-tee) the state of being poor

FIND OUT MORE

BOOKS

Kjelle, Marylou Morano. *The Quest to End World Hunger*. Hockessin, DE: Mitchell Lane Publishers, 2015.

Senker, Cath. *Poverty and Hunger*. Mankato, MN: Smart Apple Media, 2012.

Spilsbury, Louise. *Humanitarian Aid Worker*. New York: Rosen Publishing Group, Inc., 2015.

WEB SITES

Kids Can Make a Difference—What Kids Can Do
kidscanmakeadifference.org/what-kids-can-do
Learn how to do your part to help fight hunger.

Oxfam—"Everybody Eat, Drink, Earn, and Learn"
www.oxfam.org.uk/what-we-do/content/everybody-eat
Watch a short video that shows how Oxfam changes lives around the world.

INDEX

24

ABOUT THE AUTHOR

Katie Marsico is the author of more than 200 children's books. She lives in a suburb of Chicago, Illinois, with her husband and children.